Robin Tayla

Ian McElhinney was born in Belfast, 1948. He was educated at Belfast Royal Academy and Friends's School Lisburn. After studying sociology and politics in Scotland and the United States, he began his acting career in 1978 and is well-known for his work on television, film and in the theatre.

.

THE GREEN SHOOT

THE GREEN SHOOT

*a one-man show based
on the life & writings of John Hewitt
and the diaries of his wife, Roberta*

devised and compiled by
IAN McELHINNEY

LAGAN PRESS
BELFAST
1999

Published by
Lagan Press
7 Lower Crescent
Belfast
BT7 1NR

© The estate of John Hewitt, 1999
Compilation and arrangement of material © Ian McElhinney, 1999

The moral right of the author has been asserted.

ISBN: 1 873687 46 X
Author: McElhinney, Ian
Title: The Green Shoot
1999

Cover Photo: Ian McElhinney as John Hewitt
in Tinderbox Theatre Company's production of *The Green Shoot*
(*reproduced courtesy of Tinderbox Theatre Company. Photo by Phil Smyth*)
Cover Design: December Publications
Set in New Baskerville
Printed by Noel Murphy Printing, Belfast

to the memory of
Esta McElhinney

THE GREEN SHOOT
(1997)

The Green Shoot was commissioned by the John Hewitt International Summer School and was devised and compiled by Ian McElhinney. It was first presented at the 10th John Hewitt International Summer School on 26th July, 1997.

Produced by Tinderbox Theatre Company, the play received its first professional production on 6th May 1999 at the Ardhowen Theatre, Enniskillen.

Director	Stephen Wright
Stage Manager	Marianne Crosslé
Technical Stage Manager	John Riddell
Outreach Officer	Nuala Reilly
Producer	Eamon Quinn

ACT ONE

HEWITT:

Taste ... taste ... Belfast, 1984. Lord Mayor, members of the Council, and friends. You will appreciate that this is a remarkable day for me. A unique day. Becoming a freeman of my native city is indeed a remarkable experience. And therefore anything I say can be none other than highly personal. But, if my name is to be remembered, I should like it to be in the words of little Dr. William Drennan of Cabin Hill. I should like his words to be somehow associated with me. He described himself as:

A man of taste more than talent,
Not learned, though of letters,
His creed without claws
And his faith without fetters.

The faith I have always sought has been inclusive not exclusive. But various creeds have claws, and faiths fetters, like those fundamentalists of all persuasions, for instance that loathsome ideologue, Dr. Henry Cooke, one of the burn again people.

HENRY COOKE:

Presbyterians, I speak to you. The Bible and its principles have influence over you. The spirit that descended upon John Knox has influence over you. Gone are the days, when in Ireland Wentworth unleashed his bloodhounds on the track of your fathers. Look at the city of Belfast. Look at our prosperity now. All this we owe to the Union and, throned above, to the genius of Protestantism. We will guard that Union, we will guard our liberties, and secure the prosperity of our country.

HEWITT:

I do not pitch my voice
that every phrase be heard
by those who have no choice:
I write for my own kind,
their quality of mind
must be withdrawn and still,
as moth that answers moth
across a roaring hill.

I am totally opposed to all organised religions, Catholic or Protestant. I dare not call myself a Christian, yet my mind and temperament is non-conformist, protestant, dissenting. I once asked my father in what, exactly, he believed. He replied, 'In the Religion of All Sensible Men'. When I asked him to define it more closely, he rebuked me gently, 'We dare not. We are, after all, sensible men.'

It is not necessary that a writer live and die in the house of his fathers, but he ought to feel that he belongs to a recognisable focus in place and time. He must have ancestors, not just of the blood, but also of the emotions, of the quality and slant of mind. He must know where he comes from and where he is: otherwise how can he tell where he wishes to go? I have such ancestors.

William Drennan, son of a Belfast clergyman, democrat and republican and founder-member of the United Irishmen.

WILLIAM DRENNAN:

I should much desire that a Society were instituted in this city—the Brotherhood its name—the Rights of Men and the Greatest Happiness of the Greatest Number its end—its general end Real Independence to Ireland, and Republicanism its particular purpose—its business every means to accomplish these ends as speedily as the bigotry of the land we live in would permit

HEWITT:

James Hope, Jemmy Hope, a proletarian from Mallusk. His father was a Highlander, a refugee, one of the Covenanters.

JAMES HOPE:

It was my settled opinion that the condition of the labouring class was the fundamental question at issue between the rulers and the people ... As a people, we were excluded from any share in framing the laws by which we were governed. The higher ranks usurped the exclusive exercise of that privilege by force, fraud and fiction. By force the poor were subdued; by fiction the titles of the spoilers were established; and by fraud the usurpation was continued.

HEWITT:

John Mitchel, whose father was a Presbyterian minister.

JOHN MITCHEL:

Whatever god or demon may have led them first to these shores, the Anglo-Irish and Scottish Ulstermen have now far

too old a title to be questioned. A deep enough root those
planters have struck into the soil of Ulster, that it would now be
ill-striving to unplant them.

HEWITT:

So I, because of the buried men
in Ulster clay, because of rock and glen
and mist and cloud and quality of air, I am
as native in my thought as any here.

John Mitchel was a radical dissenter. He ended up as a militant
Irish nationalist who turned Catholic. Well, to me, that's not
true Dissent; that's mirror-image. True Dissent must transcend,
not substitute. There is no bolt-hole for the Dissenter.

But Mary Ann McCracken, that's my kind of person, her own
woman in every word and act.

Mary Ann taught for years in an undenominational Sabbath
School in Frederick Street; relieved the indigent; took up the
cause of Temperance; of the chimney-sweeps. She could not
take her ease. People had grown careless or forgetful. Somebody
must hold up the torch.

MARY ANN MCCRACKEN:

Belfast, once so celebrated for its love of liberty, is now so sunk
in the love of filthy lucre that there are but 16 or 17 female anti-
slavery advocates, and not one man, and none to distribute
papers to American Emigrants, but an old woman within 17
days of 89.

HEWITT:

So she shuffled to her place on the draughty quayside and handed out her leaflets.

One who directly sought to influence me was Dr. Alexander Irvine, the author of *My Lady of the Chimney Corner*. He was born into poverty in Antrim in 1863. He emigrated to New York and found his way into mission work in the Bowery. Later, he became a famous public lecturer, occasionally returning to his native province. I heard him first in 1926.

He came back in 1934 to engage in a temperance campaign in a suburban Presbyterian church and once again I attended. Deeply stirred by the sermon and the preacher, I wrote a pair of sonnets dedicated to him and posted them off.

Now, Harry Midgley, the radical socialist, was a fervent admirer of Irvine and persuaded him to give an address in the Labour Hall. Well, this was something of a break with tradition. I knew others must have known from Irvine's book, *From The Bottom Up*, that he was a socialist, but during his previous visits no echo of that ugly word was ever heard. So, in the small room at the back of the Labour Hall in York Street, I was introduced to the great man. With a firm handshake, he said, 'John, those are the finest sonnets written in Ulster in the last fifty years'. Across my mind flashed the cynical thought: How could you know? Have you ever read Herbert Moore Pim or Archbishop Alexander? And, if not, how dare you dogmatise? But I thrust these flickers aside. The remark, unimportant in itself, was typical of the man. Every sentence was to him an assertion, a gesture.

That night, Irvine spoke of social justice and the historical role of the Christian church in relation to it, of the Agitator Christ and the communism of the early disciples.

This was a new, a greater Irvine. This was the man who had exposed the outrages of the chain gangs in the southern states, who had stood shoulder-to-shoulder with Jack London in the American Socialist Party. And all of us listening were swept up in the tides of history.

DR. ALEXANDER IRVINE:

This, then, is the betrayal of the organised church. That she fell on her knees before the Emperor and has been kneeling ever since. Yet this too is our responsibility. We cannot stand outside and mock. We have each of us in our hearts to effect the great reconciliation of the social protest and the Christian dynamic. And it might be that, before Christianity among men becomes an active polity, the organised church must perish.

HEWITT:

Well, of course, there was trouble afterwards. The popular smiling public man had turned traitor. He had savaged the ideals of his sponsors, the YMCA and the Presbyterian Church. He had violated the Rotarian Code. He had taken the Lord's name in vain. He had consorted with atheists and communists and the newspapers had reported it. The row in the YMCA had been terrific. Resignations were threatened, withdrawals of support, 'if that monster were ever again allowed to darken its doors'. Even the Unionist Headquarters in Glengall Street had weighed in with its stern warning. So this was Irvine's last public appearance in the city.

But, on a later private visit, he told me that he no longer felt he was in a false position. He was a free man with no necessity for compromise. There were unpopular things to be said in Ulster, values to be maintained. He would do what he could, but his health was poor, his home base was thousands of miles away in California. Someone was needed to say the unpopular things, to maintain the imperilled values.

That someone was me.

Why? Perhaps because of some of my emotional ancestors. Perhaps because of my personal ancestors. I was greatly influenced by my father, Robert Telford Hewitt. He was a teacher, in fact the headmaster of a church primary school.

Walking to school with my father every day
as man with man, gave me a striding mind.
We talked of everything, of Bible stories,
if they were true or false or possible?
What would Home Rule mean if it came about?
Why are some politicians known as Tories?
How many rainless days become a drought?
Could God our Father send a soul to Hell?
This private class for one was everyday
my seminar, my university,
my asking answered in a friendly way
where heaven was? Why leaves fall from a tree?
And rainbows, tides, eclipses, falling stars?
Who was Jack London? Who was C.B. Fry?
Why are they fighting in the Balkan Wars?
His answers framed to stretch my inching wit

he so contrived to set my doubts at ease.
I sometimes think romantically of it
as walking with the shade of Socrates.

For some years before I was born, my father had great difficulties
with the cleric who was his school manager. He was so convinced
of this man's duplicity he decided he was not fit to baptise me.
He could not easily call on the services of any other cleric, and,
anyhow, rated the convention so unimportant that I was never
baptised.

Add to this the fact that, since our family doctor had no great
belief in vaccination, and deliberately used an innocuous
concoction which left no scar, I have often felt myself doubly
free from the twin disciplines of organised religion and science.
I can quite honestly cry a plague on both your houses.

Plague, a strange word that, plague. My great-grandmother
died of a plague, of a fever in fact caught in the Famine year of
1847 over the half-door of her house from a starveling beggar.

There's not a chance now that I might recover
one syllable of what that sick man said,
tapping upon my great-grandmother's shutter,
and begging, I was told, a piece of bread;
for on his tainted breath there hung infection
rank from the cabins of the stricken west,
the spores from black potato-stalks, the spittle
mottled with poison in his rattling chest;
but she who, by her nature, quickly answered,
accepted in return the famine-fever;

and that chance meeting, that brief confrontation,
conscribed me of the Irishry forever.

By such things is one defined. These then are some of my
ancestors, and I, I am the Green Shoot, asking for the flower.

ROBERTA:

My name is Roberta Black. I was born in 1904. We came to live
at 48 Agnes Street, Belfast, in 1907. The Hewitts were amongst
our neighbours. My father, Robert Shephard Black, had a little
shop which mostly did watch repairs. He became an alcoholic
and died in 1915. My mother took on a shop herself but she was
not a first-rate businesswoman and struggled on, eventually re-
marrying in the 1930s. In 1929, I emigrated to Canada and in
1930 to New York. I came home for a holiday in 1933 and met
Johnny Hewitt.

HEWITT:

I re-met Ruby, childhood's friend, established an honest physical
relationship on a free basis of mutual regard.

My dear Ruby

I shall, will, must, cannot do other than see you tomorrow
night, despite your evasions. Ring me to decide a plan of
campaign. Yours with a hug and a kiss, not to mention a
bruise or two. John

Only when our relationship deepened in significance did we
consider marriage. That was in 1934. That started a share of
problems of its own. It took nearly two years of living together
for us to reach equilibrium.

Dear Ruby

I read in bed last night quite a while. I remembered the last time I'd been there. I missed you. It was 11.30 when I couldn't get on with the book for thinking of you. My loneliness, appalling, begs for mirth to ease its sorrow. So ...

I don't believe I'll ever write respectable prose again
I'll only need to catch a sight of this wonderful world of men
And I go spinning and somersaulting
Touching my toes and neatly vaulting
By the thought of them
I am taught of them
Not to be solemn and grim.
The curse of Adam is
And of Madam is
God wanted a limerick, but just got a hymn.

Them's heroic couplets, iambic pentameter—you might say—or then again you might not.

ROBERTA:

Oh Johnny! Some people, on first acquaintance, are shy of Johnny, like Maureen, Patrick Maybin's wife, for instance. It's a pity he has such a haughty exterior. It's just because he is shy himself. I try to soften him. I said to him once 'You never describe me in any of your poems, except 'The Little Lough'— 'your pale face'. Well, now I have a much better colour and it should be changed to 'your red face'. He gave one of his crackling loud bursts of laughter and said he could never get conceity with me, because I mocked his poems.

We shared the same political beliefs. We were both active in the Belfast Peace League. We were involved with the National Council for Civil Liberties. We committed ourselves to the investigation of that idiosyncratic piece of Stormont legislation, the Special Powers Act.

In 1938, or thereabouts, we worked very hard for aid to Spain against Franco. It was not a popular cause here. But we collected a shipload of clothes and food and medical aid. For a couple of years, we kept a house full of refugees in Duncairn Gardens, the Red House. Our government wouldn't allow them to work here.

HEWITT:

There was one boy—Josifa—who was a lovely singer. He refused to go to a concert on Sunday night unless he had been to Mass first. Of course, all the local hosts were freethinkers or atheists. They wouldn't take him. So I took him to St. Patrick's. I was the only one prepared into go to a Catholic Church. Well, it meant nothing to me.

During all of this time I was working as art assistant at the Belfast Museum and Art Gallery. I wasn't involved in buying pictures then. It was the curator who did that. He had no taste whatsoever. In fact, the municipal taste in pictures was represented by the Lord Mayor, one Crawford McCullough, an ignoramus of the deepest dye. I remember once, at a meeting of the North West Federation of Museums, he was making the welcoming speech, and, to show that he was acquainted with the arts, he said he 'went with Mariah, my wife, Lady McCullough, to see the great Chinese exhibition in London and, coming down the steps out

of it, she said "Crawford, is there a thing in there that you'd give
tuppence for?" and I said "No, there is not".' This same
exhibition had been described by *The Times* as one of the great
spiritual experiences of our epoch.

When Belfast Castle fell into the custody of the Corporation, I
hung some good quality reproductions up. A day or two before
it was to be formally opened, Crawford McCullough came up
to cast his austere glance over the achievement. Well, when he
saw the pictures, 'I demand that that rubbish be removed'. So
that rubbish was. Monet, Manet, Renoir, Pissaro. Unlike
Crawford McCullough I was not inoculated against art—
organised religion and science yes, art, no.

Ruby has gone to Carnlough for a rest and I am alone with the
radio and incessant reports of mobilisations and men marching
to frontiers. We have just sent the Spanish kids back to England,
purged our hearts of the intimate griefs of Spain and now
another horror has broken. World War Two. I know that
anything these days is overshadowed and outshone by the
shape of events, and one man's efforts and interests looks tiny
and insignificant against the terror of clashing forces. Yet I talk
and talk everywhere I am asked for. People need help and
guidance and for art there just isn't anybody else to give it. I
have chosen this eunuch role and must abide the consequences.

Just listen to my diary.

Yesterday, I spoke to soldiers in the country and shared the
subsequent horrors of the mess. The captains talked about
shooting. The majors apologised for the food. The colonel,

discussed the USSR, beer, cubism and all-round-goodness-at-sport. They frightened me with their hierarchy and good form.

Last night I gave my WEA usual on Watteau and the French 18th century. The audience took the lovely whores' bottoms and bosoms very well indeed. You see, 'It is Art'.

Last Thursday, I adjudicated an oratory competition for a Young Farmers' Club at Boardmills. It was the most hopeful experience I've had in years. They all believe that social changes are essential. They were earnest, serious, logical and young: and of both sexes. Even in these black days, there is a gleam of dawn and not where we, in our sophistication, expected.

I was at Ballywalter Young Farmers' Club. The more I see of these the better I like them. If the young people of Ulster get a chance, they'll be alright. Our biggest problem here is the absolute absence of a competent alternative to the official groups. The Nationalists are sectarians, The Independents are a parasitic growth on the Orange Lily. The Labour Party shows no great liveliness.

I was in Dublin for a couple of days. I had to meet a group of modernist artists. O boy! I had hoped their pictures would be Symbolist in manner, but Irish in content. Instead, they were bogus, naive, sterile abstractions, utterly irrelevant to place or time. I can't give my blessing to an art that despises communication. There was more hope in Ballywalter when I heard a discussion on the technique of ploughing matches.

All this travelling to and fro didn't agree with me. I became hysterical at even the most distant prospect of a bore bearing down the platform. I hid in books. I caught later trains. I walked the long way round. I became a mentally unfit person.

Last Tuesday, I spoke on Irish painting to the Young Ulster Society. On Friday, to the Russia Today Society on Soviet art. On Saturday, a meeting here with Boyd and McFadden to decide the future of the arts magazine *Lagan*. This morning, an Arts Council committee meeting; this afternoon, an exhibition in Ewarts factory. And tonight, I have just come back from a lecture on Marxism to a church guild. So it goes on, well meant but irrelevant. Next Saturday forenoon, I give the last lecture of the season. Next year, I shall be more sparing of my appearances. I have decided to cultivate my own garden. I have a fantastic notion that poetry matters. If I am to be remembered at all, it will be for verse. Yes! If I am to be remembered, it will be for verse.

My father has been bed-fast for two years, but now the general election is here, he insists my sister help him to the polling-booth across the road. You see, it was always important to vote. I can remember when my parents' votes were stolen, because they were known as 'disloyal' people. They weren't unionists, you see. My father was a Home Ruler. Well he did vote. He voted against Churchill. It was almost his final act.

I regret the veils of difference which flickered between us—not emotionally, but theologically. But I can't help recognising that, whatever may be the end of man, he is safe. His charity and tolerance frequently annoyed me. His puritanism astounded;

and his general goodwill, exemplified in good works, humbled me. To have believed in the innate goodness of man, to have been optimistic about the world, to have been loyal to his ideals, often at some considerable personal cost, to have worked joyously for the love of it, to have painted poorish watercolours and played the 'cello badly, is, I think, as near to the good life as most of us can get.

This was my father.
This said I have told you nothing of
the greatest man of all the men I love.
In my best moments, feeling justly proud,
I wait his smile and slow approving nod,
but suddenly I know he is not here,
and have small faith that he is anywhere,
and I must chalk the little victories
for life and art and human decencies
as if on blackboard in a public place
and never know them radically defined
by the bright lens of his translucent mind.

My father—died 1945.

ROBERTA:

It was in 1946 we started to rent the Gate Lodge to the Convent of the Sisters of St. Louis in Cushendall. We used to go there for weekends often. When we arrived, I'd light the fire, Johnny would go for water. We'd spread our blankets around to air them and then went to McDonnells at Cloughglass for milk and eggs, perhaps a pat of butter in those days of rationing. We always enjoyed the crack in McDonnells. Then we'd visit

Charlie McAuley or Dr. McSparran; or we'd see Pat O'Loan. We'd talk about the Glens and the literature of the Glens. On Sunday evenings, we'd walk down for the bus to Larne at six o'clock, for the train to Belfast, to be home by nine.

HEWITT:

We'd actually been going down there since 1940. It was the period when I first became aware of the march of the seasons, more than you would have in a city, more than the blossoms and the trees. I saw the fields change, and got closer to nature. I got to know the country people, too, and got pally with them. But there were two characters in the Glens to whom I was powerfully drawn. One was Pat O'Loan, the carpenter. I was very fond of Pat. He was a droll, quiet old man who lived alone. I remember one night as he was leaving the cottage, he was standing in the doorway saying goodbye. It was around midnight and we heard a corncrake in the low meadow, and he said, 'It's right good company'. I thought, how lonely can you get to find a corncrake company!

And Pat McDonnell. He told us one day about a man asking for jam at Stephenson's the grocer. He got a one pound pot, his ration for potato planting. Pat McDonnell said, 'I'm feared it'll no go very far unless it is like the 1lb of butter the boyo got for potato drilling. It did that, and the turf cutting, and, he said, if he had had a lint pulling it would have done that too for it was that bad nobody would have put a mouth on it'.

ROBERTA:

Walking was a great passion. One day I put some bread and cheese and a tin of honey, tea and a bottle of milk in a rucksack and we set off. We started to walk over the viaduct and up to Glendun. We looked and listened and dallied and spurted as we felt, ate wild raspberries by the score and found some fat blackberries ripe and ready. We found men working turf on the mountain and I said, 'A man at turf means something to make tea in' and went up and asked him. He had a lovely wee turf fire, red and warm, and gave us a large teapot and water. We spread our coats on the moss and very soon had a great feast and delicious tea. The sun came out from behind the clouds and the world was a grand place. We got back to Cushendall about four o'clock, sunned, aired and asking no more of this earth.

Now we're by the fireside and I can tell by the puffs of Johnny's pipe and the paper and the pencil, that he's onto a poem and it won't come right. When I lift my head, his eyes are always fastened on me. It used to disturb me, but now I know his old head is churning and I am a live anchor for his eyes.

We love this wee place, in hail or shine, and I sometimes wonder if I will have to pay yet for the good life I have. Socially or financially, we are no place, but very often I realise, in Johnny, and in the rich interest life has for us I am wealthy and do not deserve to get life so easy. Often Johnny says to me in the cottage, 'We are the lucky ones'.

HEWITT:

Yes, we were lucky. We had great times in the Glens, we had great pals there. We pulled flax together, lifted potatoes and worked in the hay fields. But I discovered that I wasn't one of them. I knew I couldn't become one of them, because there were too many hedges between us.

Frankly, I was appalled by their limitations. That's one of the things that keeps me from being a 105 per cent Irishman—the fact that part of my tradition is a British democratic one. I found that many of my emotional heroes, my imaginative icons, were English, from Chaucer on. Particularly the English radical tradition, the English tradition of dissent. George Fox, the first Quaker, the Levellers, the Diggers in the 17th century, Tom Paine at the end of the 18th century, and in the 19th century, William Morris.

Equally, though my sense of identity with the folk and the land may have developed from my deepening familiarity with the Glens people, my regionalism came to me largely through the American socialist, Lewis Mumford.

Trying to waken folk to the concept of the Region seemed to me the necessary first step to prise Ulster loose from the British anchorage. Then and only then, when free in ideology, could the unity with the other part of the island be realised and established. Only when the planters realise themselves for what they are for the first time, not Britain's pensioners nor stranded Englishmen and Scots, but a special kind of Irish themselves, only then could they with grace make the transition to federal unity.

I've always maintained that our loyalties had an order: to Ulster, to Ireland, to the British Archipelago, to Europe; and that anyone who skipped a step or missed a link falsified the total. The Unionists missed out Ireland: the northern

Nationalists—the Green Tories—couldn't see the Ulster under their feet; the Republicans missed out both Ulster and the Archipelago; and none gave any heed to Europe at all.

Of course, my regionalist views were never popular and, as a result, I was considered in the north a Republican and in the south a neo-Unionist.

ROBERTA:

But it amused Johnny to watch the word 'regional' catch on in the most unlikely places. The very people who told him he was 'batty' seem to be veering round. Even the BBC.

HEWITT:

But I realise now that I was quite wrong. Ireland is not a region, it is many regions.

ROBERTA:

Ever since we were married, I've tried to push Johnny to have a book published. Now, at last, we have *No Rebel Word*.

HEWITT:

I'd like to dedicate it to you. It would make sense. After all, you are the 'we' in the book.

ROBERTA:

What about your mother?

He said nothing. I knew he felt hurt by his mother's lack of interest in his poetry. She certainly thinks it is a waste of time and that there is no money in it. But I can honestly say, though

I wish we had a little more money, I would rather Johnny wrote and had his book now than £500 a year. If he gets good reviews I'll be jumping happy. Geoffrey Taylor's foreword is quite good. I felt it was a bit guarded, but Johnny said, 'No, no, it's just right. I am a minor poet.' I said in that case I would call my book *I Married a Minor.*

The book is very solemn, very pessimistic. Strange. Johnny is always so optimistic. He sometimes annoys me being so. I preach caution: 'Now, we won't count on it'. He preaches 'Not *if* I am Director of the Museum. *When!*'

HEWITT:

We were lucky in our friends. Roberta kept an open house, so even if I was working, when we had visitors she'd bring them in and give them a cup of tea. Two of my earliest and closest friends were John Luke and Billy McClughin, practical painters both. They educated me. We read all the books as they came out. I often felt myself a lightweight in their company. But we had our disagreements; for instance, I wrote to John Luke about his painting, 'Mother and Child'.

Dear Jack

I know that you won't take amiss what I am about to say. I cannot but be impressed by the technical virtuosity of your work. But as to its significance as an act of communication, I am deeply disappointed. It said nothing to my emotions.

Jack wrote back.

JOHN LUKE:

As to this coldness business, I've heard a lot about it directly and indirectly; I often wonder what it is all about. The wretched term is bandied about as if one had committed a deep moral crime. I can't be smart like the lad at the top of the class and say to you, 'Righto, John, I'll see to it that you get your spot of warmth and human feeling in the next and all the future paintings'. It's a mystery to me how it gets into a picture and just as big a mystery how it is ever left out. Warmth and human feeling is a gift from the Gods and, as they aren't bureaucrats, but grand and glorious old boys who follow a strong line of favouritism, there's not very much we can do about it.

ROBERTA:

John Luke's assurance that he is the supreme painter of his age rubs me the wrong way. He spent everyday at his exhibition, talking to everyone and explaining his pictures. I introduced him to a prim little lady who said, 'It's a lovely show.' John Luke said, 'Yes, it is.' The lady, a little primmer, said, 'Your Madonna's really a lovely picture.' John Luke said, 'Yes, it is.' Sharp look from the little lady at this stage. Where is the modesty one expects to find in great artists? The lady said, 'This is the most interesting exhibition I've seen for some time.' John Luke said, 'Yes, it is.' The lady, now very grim-faced, offered her hand and departed coolly. John Luke very happy, never noticed a thing and hugged the praise. He is so in love with himself he can talk about nothing else.

HEWITT:

Love's a strange business. You never know until it happens. I was 'in love' lots of times since I was 10, but only when the world arranged an American depression and Roberta came back to Ireland did reality emerge. Now, after over 13 years, I am continually moved by her goodness. I'm amazed at my good fortune.

ROBERTA:

It's our anniversary. We have been married for 14 years now. I am happier and more content today than ever. Our marriage has been a happy one. I am sorry we have no children, but maybe Johnny would not have enjoyed such freedom. I gave him his pen and his pencil.

HEWITT:

I wrote to my young doctor friend, Patrick Maybin, who is in a quandary over love.

My dear Patrick,

Intellectuals have a hell of a time becoming adjusted emotionally to members of the opposite sex. They are not satisfied with mere animal adaptation. They insist on mental satisfactions. I was engaged to be married to a young woman and it took me six years to outgrow the infatuation and to realise the incompatibility. I was rescued by a married woman who, decent enough, served her purpose and set me free to deal with women more easily thereafter. Your problems have only really begun. But I warn you not to be sentimental, be ruthless. Your happiness is at stake, and you must not allow part of your nature—I don't know which part has so far been involved—to distort the problem. There is no hurry. You are young, you have not yet shocked the world into saluting you. I have nine years start and the world still remains singularly unimpressed. For professional acclaim you will require many years yet of experience and there's always the daily risk of a drunk motorist, a stray piece of shrapnel, an epidemic, a bit of tainted fish or a mad barber. We must recognise the fatalities of time and chance, the events to which the act of living is now subject.

Yours John

ROBERTA:

Events, yes. Like debts, for instance. I counted up our debts after tea. Total: £67 4s 3d. Mother gave me a hundred pounds to use if we needed it and now there is only £44 left. So we owe her £56. I said to Johnny we owed £123. He said I made it appear that we were sunk and I said, 'No, we only owed £123.' I hate owing money. He says he doesn't care. I was cross with him and blamed him for not facing how we stood and drawing in our horns. I have said I won't smoke till we are clear. I won't go to the cottage because it costs nine and fivepence each in fares. I wish I could keep accounts. Now I'm miserable.

I was so miserable that I stayed in bed. Johnny brought me breakfast. Then he worked all day on his Ulster poets. I hope they are of some value to someone. I'll be glad when it's finished. Work, work, work. I am sick of all this work. There is too much work going on in this house.

All the same, I wish I had more time to write down Johnny's monologues to me. When he is really interested in something he expounds it to me in great earnestness. Sometimes when I am rushed to death trying to cook or think of what I am going to give our numerous callers to eat, I listen with one ear, then

I get some wonderful thought from him and I feel a proper Martha and I know I should listen to him and remember. He should have married a more intelligent woman. With money. But sometimes it is too much for me to be cook, cleaner, literary confidant, wife, fan and then to keep a person on the boards that is Roberta, not just Johnny's wife.

Maybe one shouldn't try. Maybe, my job is to keep the wheels greased and remain a nonentity.

Curtain

ACT TWO

HEWITT:

Bitch! You broke my glasses!

ROBERTA:

I found the bits of glass and we went home. I was sure I'd put his eye out and I was terrified. It was such an unhappy day. A Saturday at the cottage. We went to the village to have a cup of tea but Johnny was so interested in Jack McBride's hunt for some old song he seemed to forget me. So I stumped up the high street and nattered about 'I was important to me, strange as it may seem'. He said I made him numb. So I hit him a clout.

Another day. Another temper.

Johnny was listening to the radio. I was washing up. I suddenly remembered he promised to get a speaker for me in the kitchen as a present for our 14th anniversary. Of course he never did. I went in and I asked him was he going to boil the tank away, his bath was ready. We were to go out. And then he dressed in his old flannels. Well, I felt I would look silly in my new suit if he had his old things on, so I put on my old suit. Then it turned out to be such a lovely day, all the females were in frocks and I felt shabby. I could have killed Johnny.

Thank God for Jane Austen. She's a real escape from poverty and washing and old clothes. The poor in her book have £450 a year, worth three times that now. While Johnny has only £488 a year. It's not a real life at all.

Last night we talked late about our position in society. By virtue of our work we are meeting the middle class on committees. They accept you on one level, but not socially. We who come from modest parents like Sam Hanna Bell, John Boyd, John Stewart, don't seem to make common cause. The difference is largely money. Johnny and I agree we don't really care for just money and we certainly don't do anything to acquire it, but at times the lack of it is upsetting. Especially when we've been in a nice house. I must be a better wife and not grumble about not having a house. After all, we are together.

Together, yes, but my time slips on alone. Reading, darning Johnny's socks, listening to the radio, listening to what he needs to read to me. Me! I'm not a reliable person. I'm throughother, mentally and physically. I'm not a very good housekeeper and no use at anything else. But I wouldn't like to be without Johnny. I suppose if I had married a plumber, I might have been happier, unaware of creative people. But I remember again walking to work with Peggy, my sister, and talking about who we would like to marry. I said I would like to marry an author and I would put up with all the queerness he would have so long as he could write and I would look after him. So here I am with Johnny. And although I bother him and pull him to bits, I always keep quiet and look after him when he is writing. Just now he is writing the short lives of his Ulster Poets and he never lets up and each night I have to listen to what he has written. Sometimes, if I'm reading, I wish Francis Davis's or Miss Balfour's old book was in the ashcan. But Johnny never notices, Even if he does, he just reads on. I sometimes think he just likes to hear himself. He must always tell somebody what he found out and usually I am the only one to tell. God help him.

However, he does pay more and more attention to suggestions from me. He read me a broadcast speech which was very emotional. Well he could hardly read it to me for almost weeping. I'm afraid I laughed at him. Rightly or wrongly, I was the means of a lot of emotion being taken out. I don't think one should be ashamed of emotion, but I feel, if it is too obvious, it puts people off.

That reminds me of Cherith Boyd. She dropped in with Rowel Friers. She was very pleased to meet Johnny, asked his opinion about art and poetry, hung on his every word. But she makes the most awfully fatuous remarks. Johnny had a very nice new pair of shoes and she said, 'Oh, Mr. Hewitt, your feet look like an advertisement for shoes. They're lovely. It must be lovely to have such nice, big, strong feet. Don't you think so, Mrs. Hewitt?' I was absolutely bursting, but refrained from saying anything other than 'Having big feet myself, I don't'. Which brought down compliments on my feet. But she sat and just gazed at Johnny in close-up, film-like admiration. He really loved it. I was quite surprised. I suppose he's the age for requiring admiration from young girls. You never know your man.

I must confess I had pangs of something akin to jealousy and wondered if this could develop. But I told myself this would be good for him and he had been very long-suffering with me when I was a bit infatuated with Robert McCoubrey in 1939. Robert came along at a time when I was finding sheer intellectual life a bit of a strain and he took me out in his car and bought me nice meals and wine and boxes of chocolates. And he was just good fun. So, I owe Johnny a bit of fling. But it has come at the wrong time for me, when I am losing my looks, and want Johnny's undivided attention. I think all this tiredness I am feeling is the beginning of the menopause.

HEWITT:

I'd like to ask Cherith Boyd down to the cottage for the weekend.

ROBERTA:

Alright.

I wasn't happy, but I said nothing. Down at the cottage, Cherith Boyd was apt to pose on the old tree stump and stand up on the skyline, just for effect, I'm sure. She was googling stupidly at Johnny. So, after lunch, I went off and lay for over an hour in a hayfield. When I came back to the cottage, Johnny was reading poetry to her and she again posed up at the skyline. I got so fed up I squealed at Johnny when he came in to help me with the tea, 'For Christ's sake, take her off that damn skyline and rape her, or whatever she wants, but just get her out of my sight till I make the tea'.

Poor old Johnny. That night, he asked me to forgive him for falling for flattery, but he thought she was interested in art and poetry and our cottage would delight her. He had been most uncomfortable in the bus on the way home, as she just sat and gazed at him all the way. I went to sleep in his arms and we said again 'And so, throughout eternity, I forgive you, you forgive me'.

But, unfortunately, I have a ghastly habit of reliving unhappy events. They sweep over me as alive as they ever were. I allow the elements to have their way with me. As Willa Muir said, 'Poets teach in verse what their wives learn in despair'.

Johnny has just drafted a note to Professor Baxter in Queen's asking if he would accept his Ulster Poets for an MA. I've been trying to get this done, but he is diffident about a degree. But I know he would like it published and this is, maybe, a way. Secretly, I feel, if he had his MA before Mr. Stendall retires from the Museum, it would count with the City Fathers in favour of his getting the directorship there.

He would like the job, I know he would, but he says he's only interested in the gallery.

HEWITT:

In the early 50s we had a Yeats exhibition. I tried to get the Committee to buy a Jack Yeats, a small one, for three hundred pounds. Tommy Henderson, who was a member of the Committee, said, 'Mr. Chairman, will the keeper of the gallery please tell us what that works out per square inch?' I said, 'Sir, I am not a quantity surveyor'. He then appealed to the Chairman for 'protection from the insults of officers'. Needless to say, we didn't get that Yeats.

As ever, the municipal taste in pictures was represented by the
Lord Mayor, then a man called Johnson. He had a detached
retina. That may have been a help. He also had an American
wife. I got to know them, to know their 'aesthetics'. He liked
pictures with distance in them. That was his sole criterion: 'It
must have distance.' She liked pictures in black frames. They
were barbarians.

ROBERTA:
They weren't the only ones ...

John Luke's mural which Johnny worked so hard to commission
was handed over to the city by the Vice-Chancellor, Dame Dera
Parker in the chair. Johnny was invited but never mentioned.
Not even on the platform. I was not even invited. After, Mr.
Frankl, a great patron of the arts and a good friend, said to me:
'Please explain me. Dame Dera said, "Mr. Vice-Chancellor is
very clever, wonderful person. He came to Belfast and we get
this great painting." Vice-Chancellor said, "Dame Dera is a
great patron of the art and she paint the mural." John Luke is
no place and this mural is the idea of one man and one man
only, and this man fought for all this all the way and this man
is John Hewitt and he is never mentioned!'

I remember too at the meeting to arrange the 1951 exhibition,
Johnny said the Ulster show should surely have an Ulster
flavour for we are not a suburb of London nor an extension of
Yorkshire, but a different people with our own speech and
characteristics and our arts must have a show, just as Wales and
Scotland. The Minister for Education, Hall Thompson, went
turkey-red and said to the organisers, 'You need not answer

that, Mr. Barry, the meeting is closed.' After, at tea, he would not speak to Johnny. It must be difficult for the authorities to think that an Ulsterman could have a great affection for Ulster without hating England or, for that matter, Eire.

Prof. Baxter has just rung Johnny to say his thesis on Ulster Poets was successful and his Master of Arts secure. I didn't doubt it for a minute, really.

Johnny hadn't told anyone in the gallery that he was doing his thesis, so the MA came as a great surprise. He told Mr. Stendall first and then he told the councillors. There was a letter of congratulations from the City Hall via the Town Clerk. Mr. Frankl says Johnny must use all his charm and cunning to work himself in as director when Stendall goes. Poor old Johnny has no cunning and not much charm, at least not any he can turn on to order. He's much too honest. Mr. Frankl says that Johnny must be careful what he says on air as some people think he is a communist. Mr. Frankl has promised to find us a house and lend us a deposit—about £600. I wouldn't take it, but it was very nice of him.

I'm afraid I phoned an estate agent. He showed me three houses. I got awfully fed up with the flat when I got back. I started to yap about Johnny not allowing me to buy him a house ages ago. I behaved very badly.

HEWITT:

In 1952, Sidney Stendall was due to retire as director of the Belfast Art Gallery and Museum, and I expected, as did others, that I might be appointed. I had the experience, and the qualifications. I was the only applicant who had a university degree, who had travelled abroad, who had published papers on art and in professional journals both here and abroad.

From the candidates assembled, an odd bundle of disengaged clergymen and others scarcely any better qualified, only one name emerged as a possible rival. W.A. Seaby, FSA, Curator of Taunton Castle Museum. It seemed odd therefore that, in the prolonged interval between application and interview, the Director should make a special journey to Taunton to inspect the Castle Museum's eligibility for a development grant. I need hardly say that it was not from the Director that I learned of this trip.

Less than a week before the interviews were eventually to take place, the phone rang. A very guarded voice enquired if I were I. I was. If I could guess who was speaking. I could. Something greatly to my disadvantage had blown up. Could I possibly leave the Gallery for a short time this afternoon? About three? It would be better for us not to be seen together. Could I be on the Lagan at the end of the King's Bridge at three then? Now, I have never believed in secret societies for, as Jamie Hope said, 'Oaths will never bind knaves'. However, I took up my position at the time appointed. The car passed and pulled up fifty yards on. I followed and got in. My fellow conspirator murmured 'We can't talk here. Let's go somewhere safe'. We drove to a cul-de-sac of newly built, as yet unoccupied, houses, and stopped. Then he unwound his story. The Chairman—a Mr. Tougher, golfer, shirt-manufacturer, son of a once well-known pawnbroker in the city and inevitably a Unionist—was going round the City Hall showing council members a letter he had received from Mrs. Mary O'Malley. She was a member of the Irish Labour Party which provided about half-a-dozen councillors representing wards with strongly Catholic populations. In the letter she stated that, as she could not be present at the next meeting of the committee, she wished to be recorded as supporting me. This was a personal letter to the Chairman but he was making more than private use of it. Tougher was asserting that I was a communist and, in addition, that I was 'one of the Tomelty clique'. Joseph Tomelty was just then starring in an American play in the West End. He was a well-known member of the Group Theatre Company and a contributor to the arts magazine, *Lagan*. As one of those most vitally concerned with the arts, I could not help knowing him; but that, of course, was my offence.

This then was the situation. Allegations were being widely-canvassed among the people in whose hands the appointment lay. My informant could do no more, I must shift for myself as best I could. This was the epoch when McCarthyism was in the news: guilt by association; the smear; the lie. I could not help feeling a sort of identification with its victims. In any society with standards of public decency, this sort of thing could not, should not happen. I was in a state of turmoil but that evening Roberta and I set about trying to stem the attack. I went out to call on W. R. Gordon, my only personal friend on the committee.

ROBERTA:

I went to see Stuart K. Henry, an elderly councillor I knew. He confirmed that he saw the letter and was perturbed as up to that time his vote was for Johnny. I explained to him that Johnny was a socialist, not a communist, and he promised his support.

Johnny's interview was on Friday at 10.15am. Just as he was leaving Mrs. Stendall phoned to wish us luck and said thát the Liverpool boat bringing Mr. Seaby, the only other candidate on the shortlist, was held up by storms and wouldn't be in until 2 o'clock.

HEWITT:

Two, right. I decided to go on anyway, so I finished dressing and went out to catch a bus. Who should be on the bus but Mr. Stendall, but he never mentioned that the boat was late.

So I had to return that afternoon. I met Bill Seaby in the members' reading room. I was called first. The Chairman asked the questions. I answered with competence. Then it was Seaby's turn. Alone in the reading room, I examined the shelf of new library books and thought that they fairly represented the taste of the City Fathers. Then Seaby returned. After a time, I shall never know of what duration, he was called in again by the committee clerk. This is the normal routine. I had lost.

I remained alone. Should I slip away? Or wait until I was formally told? I would wait, for I have a stubborn streak which makes my retreats few. Then, at the far end of eternity, the committee clerk put his head round the door and said, 'O you're still here! I suppose you know that Mr. Seaby's been appointed?' I gathered my coat and, going out of the building, encountered W.R. Gordon and Morris Harding, the old sculptor. Gordon blurted out, 'It's a bloody scandal. You were beaten by the Chairman's casting vote.' With these bitter angry words of sympathy from the two old artists, I went out to catch a bus home, and tell Roberta that what we feared had happened.

Once again the Belfast Museum and Art Gallery had an English director. Once again without a university degree.

ROBERTA:

Everything was being said to blacken Johnny in the eyes of the Unionist Party. He was unable to control staff, he had no knowledge of administration. But the greatest shock of all was that it all pointed to one man. Stendall. Stendall who said 'I will be working for you on the Council'. Stendall who had Mr. Seaby for lunch before the interview and for dinner afterwards and who is a member of the Museums Council with him. Stendall who picked Johnny's brains, for whom Johnny wrote speeches, broadcasts, reports.

I was much more upset than I should have been. I blamed Johnny for not knowing the people he was working with. I said you want to be the just and forthright person, giving your opinion and not paying much attention to people on the City Council, in fact despising them and making no effort to be nice to them. And yet you expect them to give you a job. I blamed myself for working in the Labour Party. In fact, I was utterly defeated about it. I resented the fact I would not be able to get a nice house. Johnny went to London just after that. The first trip Mr. Stendall had ever allowed him to have. It was to buy an old silver mug.

HEWITT:

I boarded ship for Liverpool, but I could not go below to my berth. Round and round the deck I marched, fighting over every known thread of the intrigue. Once I stopped at the rail and looked down at the troubled waters, sliding, folding over, turning past and, for a minute or more, I was nearer suicide than I shall ever be again.

The next day I had lunch with Howard Sargeant, who had made generous reference to my verse in his 'Cumberland Wordsworth'. Having heard my story, he remarked, 'John, if I were you I'd get out of that God-forsaken hole'.

ROBERTA:

I went to town and bought the papers. The *Whig* reported that Chairman Councillor Tougher said in reply to the Labour Party that he had known one-and-a-half years ago that Johnny would not be a suitable director. I nearly cried on the street when I read it.

HEWITT:

In the weeks which followed, Roberta and I felt utterly alone. Most cutting of all, when business took me into the City Hall, men in the public service whom I had known for years dodged down corridors or dived round corners to avoid me.

ROBERTA:

In October, Johnny asked Mr. Stendall to give him a reference before he left. Mr. Stendall said, 'I certainly will and you should get out. Go to England. It would be better for you.' Johnny said, 'But Mr. Stendall, this is my country and I happen to love it.' Stendall just said, 'Other Ulstermen have left it before now.' This hurt Johnny very much, that old Mr. Stendall should come here and sit for thirty years and tell Johnny to get out of the same place.

Well, at the end of the month, Johnny was appointed Deputy Director. It is now December, but I still can't get over the whole thing. The final blow was the salary for deputy was fixed at £709, a rise of £29. The £75 Mr. Stendall said that Johnny would get as Acting Deputy from February of last year was never mentioned. For the first time in my life I spent money that we didn't have and December was the tightest month we ever had. With Christmas coming, too. I do so love to buy presents.

HEWITT:

The appointed Englishman came. 'I know you will probably resent my coming here but I hope we will be able to work together and make the best of it,' he said. I said that I would help him all I could. There was a temptation at that time to leave, just to get out, because they didn't want me and I didn't care to work for them. But I decided no, I'd stand my ground and only leave when it suited me. Not long after the debacle, the committee visited the museum and were shown around and I insisted on Tougher introducing me to Mrs. O'Malley, first time I'd met her. Anyway, it happened so long ago. All the bastards are dead now. God, they were a dim lot.

But that débâcle was more than a sobering experience. It was a dislocating assault. My tone grew firmer, more bitter, sadder, perhaps more courageous; in fact, this was the beginning of my freedom. It was perhaps the period of my greatest influence in Belfast, for I now had the advantage of wearing a martyr's tie.

ROBERTA:

When I get unhappy I remain most unhappy. Johnny cannot talk to me at all. He cannot help me. He's sorry for me and puts his hand on my head or kisses me. But no word or gesture is real. He never makes love to me. I'm sure this is my main trouble. He will not or cannot think this is important. On nights when I am most miserable, he lies beside me, but never a word. He goes dumb. And I go crazy. He's good and kind as he knows how, but—ah, I'm so fed up with this town. I want away, I want to run from the dragging of these our old people, from this town which won't give Johnny a good job, from poverty, scraping and old clothes. I hate everything lately. I hope to God this passes for I could not live with this utter despair. I can tell no one. I tell Johnny but he says nothing.

HEWITT:

When my father was ill, I sat for hours with him, talking about everything, purpose, value, faith, reason, progress, order, but never once, though I steered the talk as close as I might, did he ever make a frankly personal statement or even an oblique allusion to the thing that was himself. Some restraint in his character, some reticence of mind and heart, prevented him from making intimate friendships. I too have something of his restricted attitude. No one needs affection more than I. I get more than most and of the highest quality. But still the pitcher is not full.

ROBERTA:

It's awful. I'm getting old. No one looks anymore. I suppose I'm not attractive to Johnny any more. Men always show it. He never gives me hugs or kisses that are any warmer than you would give a sister. I'd much rather he would not touch me at all. I'm always hoping he will be really loving. I'm always disappointed. So now I try to protect myself by not allowing myself to be anything more than friendly. So guarded that sometimes I'm dead. I've forgotten how to be merry. We never laugh, really. We never have any ordinary fun. We can only have an intelligent conversation about dead poets. Dead Ulster poets. At times I wish their mouldy old books of miserable verse had perished! They were published. They have lasted too long! For me.

I feel I could go insane. I feel no warmth within me, make beds, cook, and wash, go to committees, talk about politics, listen to poetry. And then I explode. I hate everything actively and acutely and I shout at Johnny, 'I want someone to talk to me about me!' And then I collapse and feel small and bitchy and useless. I again sweep up the bits of my anger and put them in a dark box.

HEWITT:

Within the little house was dark with hate
and anger smashed like glass against the floor,
while that grey heifer, dawn, paused at the gate
and a bird started singing near the door.

But two in that shut house were caught and bound
in a close grapple none could disengage,
and silence, after anger, tiptoed round
through the bright spikes and splinters of their rage.

Unsleeping, each alone in time's abyss,
dealt out the hurts and shuffled them again;
in anguish clenched, what could they do but miss
day coming gently through the leaves in rain?

ROBERTA:

I read in the *Belfast Telegraph* of the death of Councillor J.P. Tougher. A jolt. My first angry thought was that it was a year too late.

However, again, I am closer to Johnny. I have realised just how good he is. I must ever remember his values are different.

He went to Coventry to interview for director of art at a new gallery there. In one way, I was sure he had it, but equally sure he'd never get the chance to leave Belfast. All our married life I wished he would get a job elsewhere, but he always gave me his talk on 'the rooted man' and I always repeated 'Roots should be under your feet, not round your neck'.

HEWITT:

When the Coventry job was advertised in 1956, I applied. I had stood my ground long enough. The salary was good. The opportunity of taking on a completely new gallery was enticing, and Coventry, with its Labour Council and their success in planning the new city, offered a congenial new context.

ROBERTA:

He rang, to say he got it. I said, 'Are you happy?' He said, 'Yes, very.'

HEWITT:

Yes, it is a most interesting place and it is growing. They don't seem to be afraid of ideas. And I like the committee that appointed me. I liked their questions. I even told them they had made a mistake in their last purchase. So in 1957 at the age of 49-plus, I went into voluntary exile.

Coventry Evening Telegraph November 2nd 1957
The future of Coventry's new Art Gallery seems to be in safe
hands. This is a conclusion that must come to anyone who
has read the policy draft put forward by the City Art Director,
Mr. J.H. Hewitt. Mr. Hewitt sensibly points out that the basic
appeal of the collection must be to the ordinary citizen.
Local painters will find in his determination to support
them the encouragement that has been lacking for so long.

Coventry is an older town than Belfast. It has a longer and very
noble, urban history. It goes back to the guilds of the Middle
Ages. But the whole city also has a feeling of rebirth. The old
cathedral and the new Basil Spence cathedral, cheek by jowl.
We have no such dramatic juxtaposition. Coventry had a sense
of the future, symbolised for me in the precinct, the fact that
the land belonged to the municipality fitted in with my ideals
of the good society, the common wealth. Being myself of the
Left, the political atmosphere here in Coventry suited me,
because Coventry has had a strong Labour council for many,
many years, and I found among the councillors many men of
integrity, something I had not experienced among local
representatives before.

There is also the odd coincidence that Hewitt is an old Coventry
name. You see, I am forever rationalising my circumstances, a
romantic at heart. I believe, however, I have become more
objective regarding my native province and my native country.
But my apparent harshness may have been partly conditioned
by the sense of rejection by my own.

A full year since I took this eager city,
the tolerance that laced its blatant roar,
its famous steeples and its web of girders,
as image of the state hope argued for,
and scarcely flung a bitter thought behind me
on all that flaws the glory and the grace
which ribbons through the sick, guilt-clotted legend
of my creed-haunted, godforsaken race.
My rhetoric swung round from steel's high promise
to the precision of the well-gauged tool,
tracing the logic in the vast glass headlands,
the clockwork horse, the comprehensive school.

Then, sudden, by occasion's chance concerted,
in enclave of my nation, but apart,
the jigging dances and the lilting fiddle
stirred the old rage and pity in my heart.
The faces and the voices blurring round me,
the strong hands long familiar with the spade,
the whiskey-tinctured breath, the pious buttons,
called up a people endlessly betrayed
by our own weakness, by the wrongs we suffered
in that long twilight over bog and glen,
by force, by famine and by glittering fables
which gave us martyrs when we needed men,
by faith which had no charity to offer,
by poisoned memory, and by ready wit,
with poverty corroded into malice,
to hit and run and howl when it is hit.

This is our fate: eight hundred years' disaster,

crazily tangled as the Book of Kells;
the dream's distortion and the land's division,
the midnight raiders and the prison cells.
Yet like Lir's children, banished to the waters,
our heart's still listen for the landward bells.

So. I keep my nostalgias, go back every year, read any book
about Ireland that I can find. Only a week or two ago, I took
down the Irish paintings from the living room walls and
replaced them with English and Scots. For I suddenly felt that
otherwise I would be unconsciously refusing a change of vision.
But it is Irish painters who hang in my study.

ROBERTA:

Here we are: Christmas 1958. A chicken came from the
McDonnells in the Glens. Twenty-four years of marriage and
we have had our first Christmas alone. Saddened by death.
Pappy, my mother, Mamma Hewitt. I didn't feel alone, so
much as—stranded. I suddenly caught sight of myself in the
mirror, a middle-aged, but active, fairly presentable woman,
when fixed-up. Married to one John Hewitt, a good man. I was
suddenly attracted to myself.

HEWITT:

I was attracted to the Midlands. After all, there are hundreds of
feuds there, too. But I was not attracted to the culture of the
motor industry. There are thousands of cars.

ROBERTA:

It's great having a wee car. It's certainly helped us to get to know
our new world.

We moved into Postbridge Road, our first house of our own, in July 1960, just before the official opening of the new gallery. As ever we had a steady stream of visitors. We had occasional lodgers, foreign students, problem children, visiting artists. We have a garden. I dug it myself. It's stuffed with things. I always overpack a garden.

HEWITT:

I know when you are at your happiest,
kneeling on mould, a trowel in your glove;
you raise your eyes and for a moment rest;
you turn a young girl's face, like one in love.

Intent, entranced, this hour, in gardening,
surely to life's bright process you belong.
I wonder, when you pause, you do not sing,
for such a moment surely has its song.

ROBERTA:

We continue our interest in politics. We were at the Aldermaston march. There was a wonderful feeling of good nature, but also of deep unity for a single purpose. The man behind was a Stalinist, another a Quaker, that old lady there was in and out of every car. Then there was the family of children in a Rolls-Royce, and a great man, Irish, who sold the *Democrat* and shouted in a rich brogue, 'We're walkin' to preserve your beautiful English villages', or to a man building a house, 'If you would build for the future, folly us'.

HEWITT:

Coventry was a Labour-controlled council, but we had Tories

on the Committee, of course. The time came when we had to
buy pictures and I wondered who would make a good start. I hit
on James Fiton, who is a left-wing man who paints pictures of
real people but in a fresh and lively style. Now, it was a big step
for working men to spend hundreds of pounds on a picture. So
I did a sales talk. The Committee fell silent. No working-class
council was prepared just to take the plunge. But one wee Tory,
who came from Cork, O'Donnell they called him, he proposed
it and another Tory seconded it, and the Labour people were
caught because they didn't want to be quoted as voting against
works of art. So, they didn't raise their voices and the picture
got through on the votes of two Tories.

ROBERTA:
In 1968, Johnny brought out his selection on William Allingham.

HEWITT:
My position is rather like that of Allingham who was, to his
chagrin, called the Poet of Bellashanny, when he dearly wanted
to be known as Irish. He wrote to Katharine Tynan about Yeats'
article 'The Poet of Ballyshannon', and said, 'Non-national
again. How sad.' He seemed to feel himself more Irish in
England than in Donegal. This I too experience.

To one living outside Ireland the impact of those terrible days
of August 1969 was heartbreaking. As I could not readily walk
among the barricades with my white flag, I found release for my
frustration in verse.

Admit the fact, you might have stood your ground
and kept one corner clear for decency,

Now, from safe distance, you assert your right
to public rage. That town is, after all,
where I was born and lived for fifty years.
I knew its crooked masters well by sight,
endured its venom and survived its sneers.
I scratch these verses on its flame-scorched wall.

ROBERTA:

Johnny cannot plan when he is retiring. He can go on until
October 1972, but he thought he would leave in March. But he
keeps changing his mind. He does not make decisions easily.
How he decided to marry me, I will never understand or know.

He is off keel and upset about Ireland and whether we return
or not. It is a most difficult time for him.

HEWITT:

Although it is my native place
and dear to me for many associations,
how can I return to that city
from my exile among strangers?
These people I now live among
are friendly in the street
and quiet in the evenings
around their own hearths.
And I grown old
do not wish to shuffle
through the rubble of my dreams
and lie down in hope's ashes:
the Phoenix is a fabulous bird.

ROBERTA:

I think retiring and going back to Ireland or staying is beyond Johnny, and also myself. Frankly, I am overpowered by the thought of moving and living on a pension in Belfast which is more expensive than here, never mind the thought of bombs and bullets. Everyone, including my sister Peggy, says we should not return. But no one knows but myself how much poetry and politics are all of Johnny's life. I cannot refuse to return. We are drowned in Irish politics as it is.

HEWITT:

You coasted along
And all the time, though you never noticed,
the old lies festered ...
You coasted along
and the sores suppurated and spread.
Now the fever is high and raging.
Who would have guessed it, coasting along?
The ignorant sick thresh about in delirium
and tear at the scabs with dirty fingernails.
The cloud of infection hangs over the city.
A quick change of wind
and it might spill over the leafy suburbs.
You coasted too long.

ROBERTA:

Johnny retires at the end of June. He hopes to return to Belfast in September. Well, he has more people to talk to in Belfast about literature. I am putting the house up for sale, reluctantly, and am not sure it is wise.

So, here we sit in 11 Stockman's Lane. Filthy. Garden, knee-high. Here we sit, listening to news bulletins. Riots. Deaths. Burnings of little houses and factories. We step from pool to pool of depression. The first church to be burned down was Paisley's. God knows where that will lead if the UVF retaliate. If they burn down a Catholic Church all Catholic Ireland will rise with the smoke of it. Johnny's sister and her husband, the Todhunters, watched a row of houses burn up the hill in Ardoyne. What a place to return to. Part of me would scamper abroad for the winter, but I know Johnny would feel a traitor in spite of the fact that his voice will go unheard by the two factions.

HEWITT:

This is my country.

Though creed-crazed zealots and the ignorant crowd,

long-nurtured, never checked, in ways of hate,

have made our streets a by-word of offence,

this is my country, never disavowed.

When it is fouled, shall I not remonstrate?

My heritage is not their violence.

ROBERTA:

It's February 1974. Johnny, well, he's enjoying retirement. I dislike being here. Sometimes, too often, I rail against this country, this house, or rather this kitchen and the fact that we can't get any jobs done or finished.

I had a dream. I was walking in a large room. I looked around and saw a group on my left. I said 'I don't know anyone here. They are all dead.' I thought 'Which of my dead I would most

like to see?' and felt it would be my mother. Then I saw a small
neat slim figure in two shades of blue and I looked and I saw
that it was my mother. And I was exquisitely happy. And I went
to her with my arms out and I said, 'Oh, Mother.'

HEWITT:

If I had given you that love and care
I long have lavished with harsh loyalty
on some blurred concept spun of earth and air
and real only in some bird or tree,
then you had lived in every pulse and tone
and found the meaning in the wine and bread,
who have been forced to walk these ways alone,
my dry thoughts droning always on ahead.
Then you had lived as other women live,
warmed by a touch, responsive to a glance,
glad to endure so that endurance give the right
to share each changing circumstance.
And yet for all my treason, you were true to me
as I to something less than you.

I have not far to journey from this place.
My home's in the rocks below there, in the bracken;
I am the foolish old man that lives in the cave.
What then to do with the narrowing years ahead?
I had hoped to die with your blessing, being old and tired.

VOICE:

First leave the cave.
Go back to men. They will listen because of your age.

HEWITT:

Bear in mind these dead:
I can find no plainer words.
I dare not risk using
that loaded word 'Remember',
for your memory is a cruel web
threaded from thorn to thorn across
a hedge of dead bramble.

I cannot urge or beg you
to pray for anyone or anything,
for prayer in this green island
is tarnished with stale breath,
worn smooth and characterless
as an old flagstone, trafficked
with journeys no longer credible
to lost destinations.

So I say only: bear in mind
those men and lads killed in the streets,
but do not differentiate between
those deliberately gunned down
and those caught by unaddressed bullets:
such distinctions are not relevant.

Bear in mind the skipping child hit
by the anonymous ricochet;
the man shot at his own fireside
with his staring family round him;
the elderly woman
making tea for the firemen